IBERIA AND ESPAÑA

TWO COMPLETE WORKS FOR SOLO PIANO

Isaac Albéniz

Dover Publications, Inc., New York

This Dover edition, first published in 1987, reproduces:
Iberia: 12 nouvelles "impressions" en quatre cahiers, as published by "Edition Mutuelle,"
Paris, in four volumes: 1ᵉ Cahier (ca. 1906), containing "Évocation," "El Puerto," "Fête-
Dieu à Séville"; 2ᵉ Cahier (ca. 1907), containing "Rondeña," "Almería" and "Triana"; 3ᵉ
Cahier (ca. 1907), containing "El Albaicín," "El Polo" and "Lavapiés"; 4ᵉ Cahier (ca.
1907), containing "Málaga," "Jerez" and "Eritaña."
España, as published by Edition Peters, Leipzig, n.d.
The original footnotes appear here in a new English translation.

Manufactured in the United States of America
Dover Publications, Inc., 31 East 2nd Street, Mineola, N.Y. 11501

Library of Congress Cataloging-in-Publication Data

Albéniz, Isaac, 1860–1909.
  [Iberia]
  Iberia ; and, España.

  The 1st work a suite.
  Reprint. Originally published: Paris : Edition Mutuelle, ca. 1906–ca. 1907 (1st work);
Leipzig : Peters, 189– (2nd work).
  Pl. no.: E.3084.M (1st work).
  1. Suites (Piano) 2. Piano music. I. Albéniz, Isaac, 1860–1909. España. 1987.
II. Title: Iberia. III. Title: España.
M22.A39I2 1987   86-755097
ISBN 0-486-25367-8 (pbk.)

CONTENTS

IBERIA

EVOCACIÓN

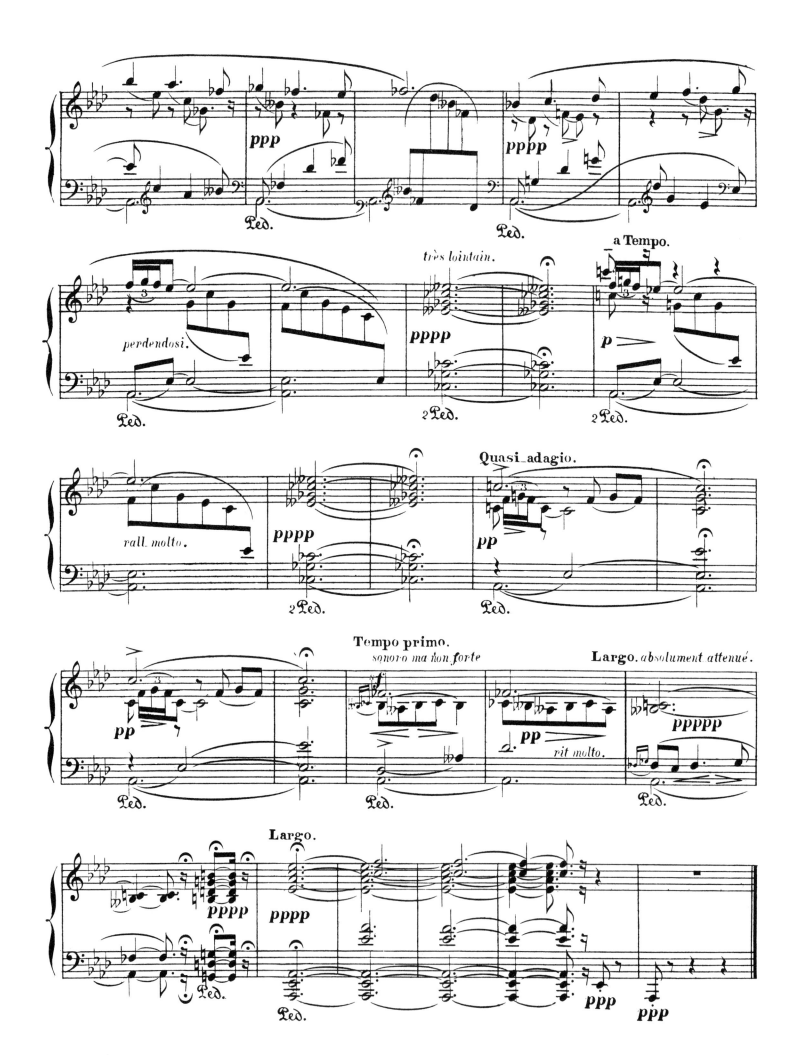

ria

EL PUERTO

EL CORPUS EN SEVILLA

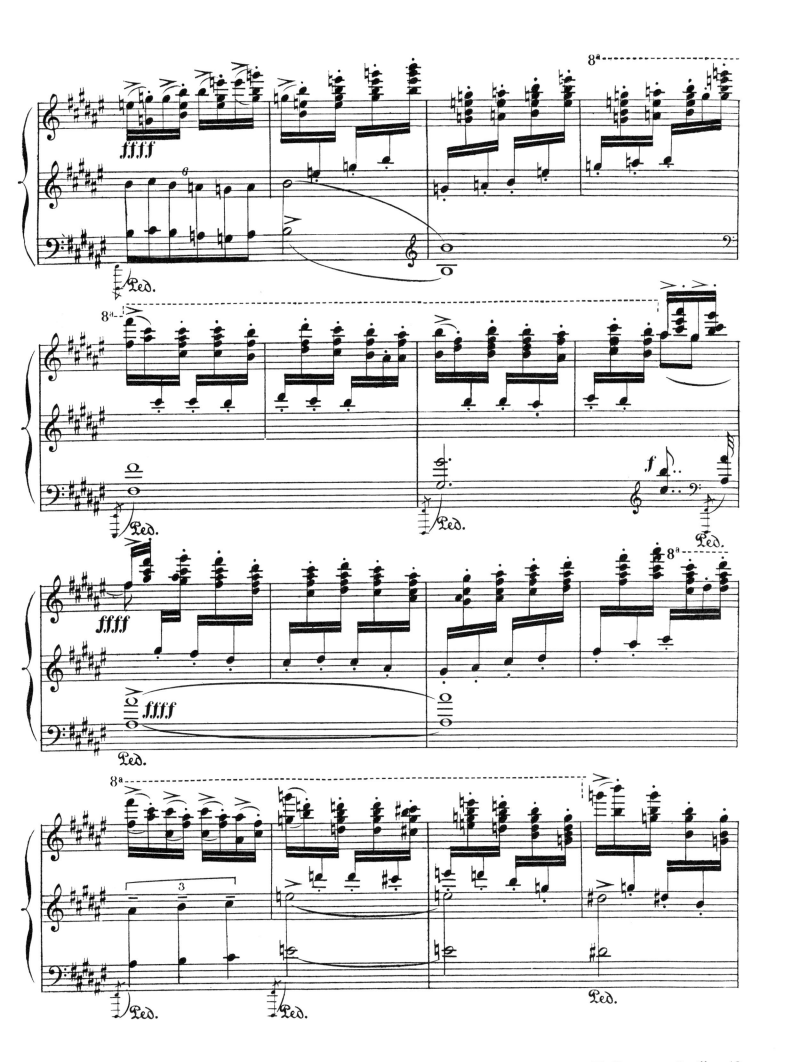

1) The fermatas with commas should be considered as actual breathing spaces.

RONDEÑA

40 *Iberia*

44 *Iberia*

ALMERÍA

TRIANA

EL ALBAICÍN*

*Gypsy quarter in Granada.

avec la petite pédale, et bien uniforme de sonorité, en
cherchant celle des instruments à anche

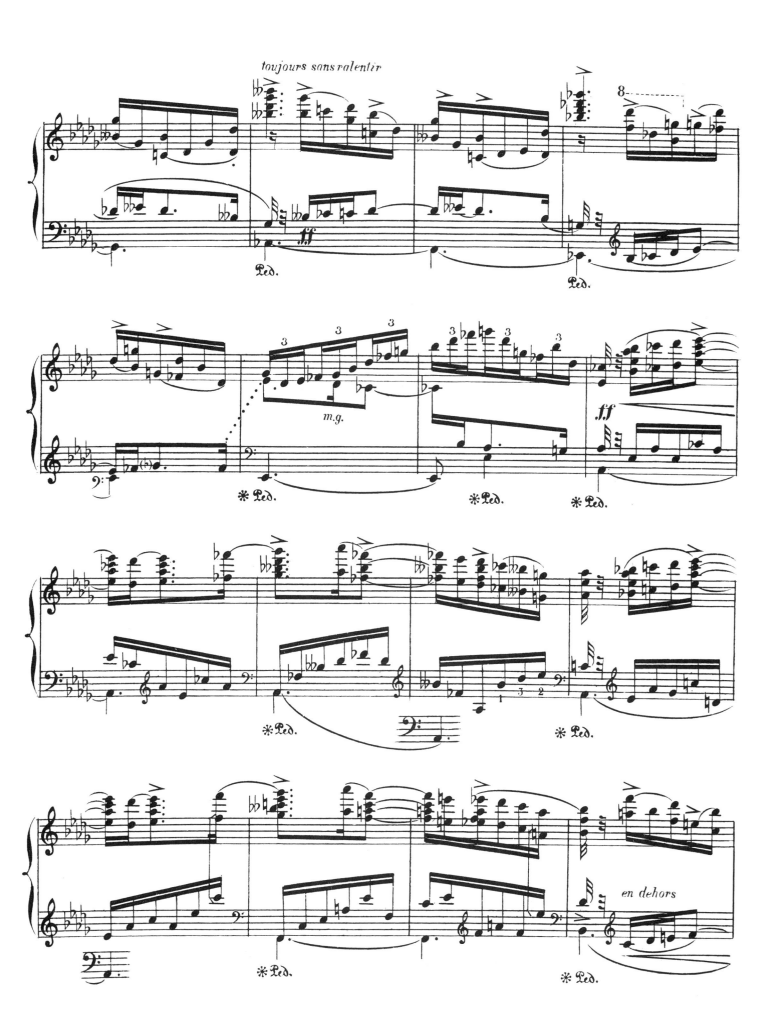

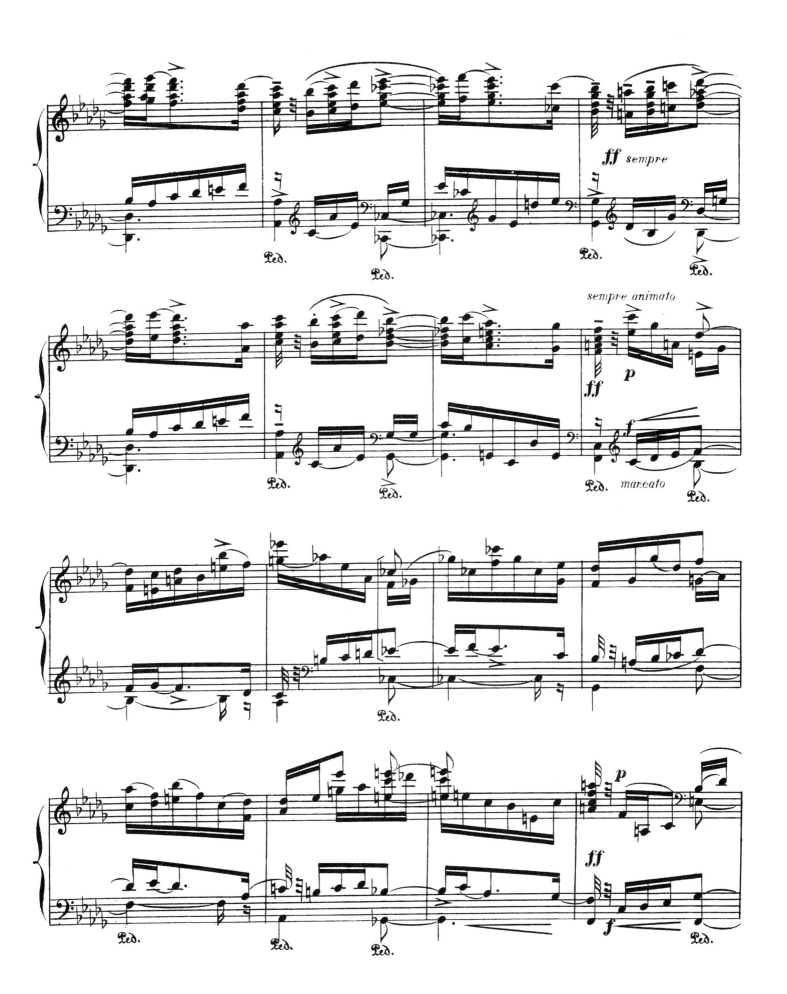

EL POLO*

*An Andalusian song and dance.

LAVAPIÉS*

Ce morceau doit être joué avec allégresse et librement

M.M. ♩ = 84 **Allegretto bien rythmé mais sans presser**

PIANO

*A working-class quarter in Madrid.

MÁLAGA

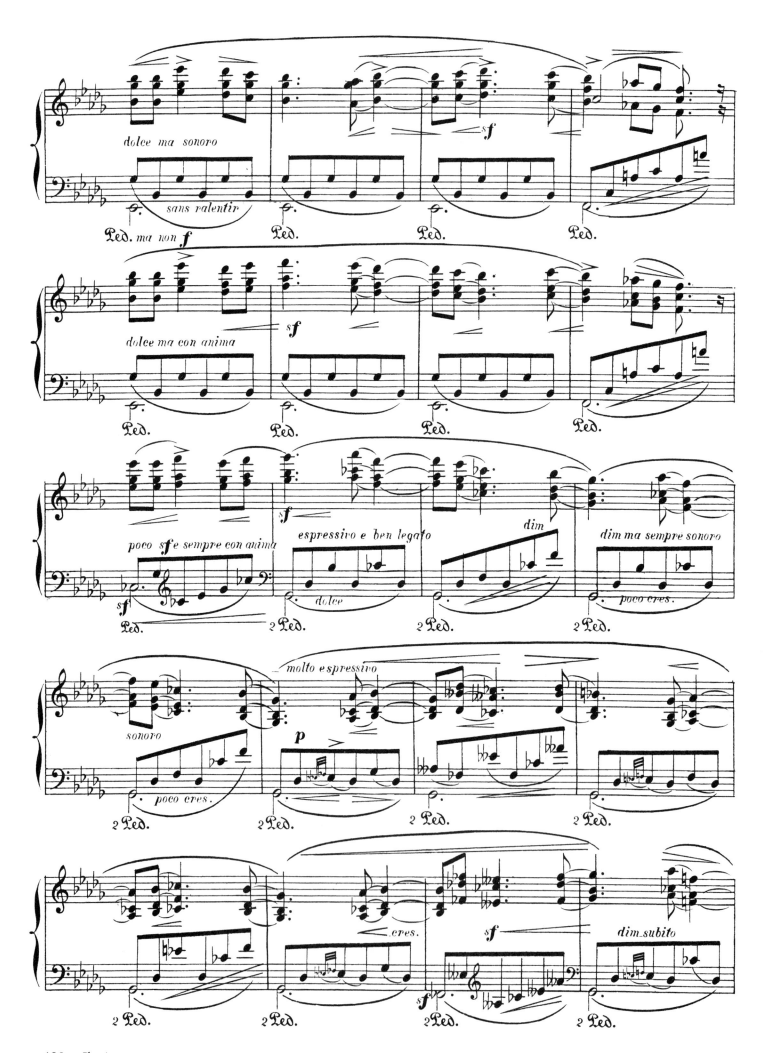

JEREZ

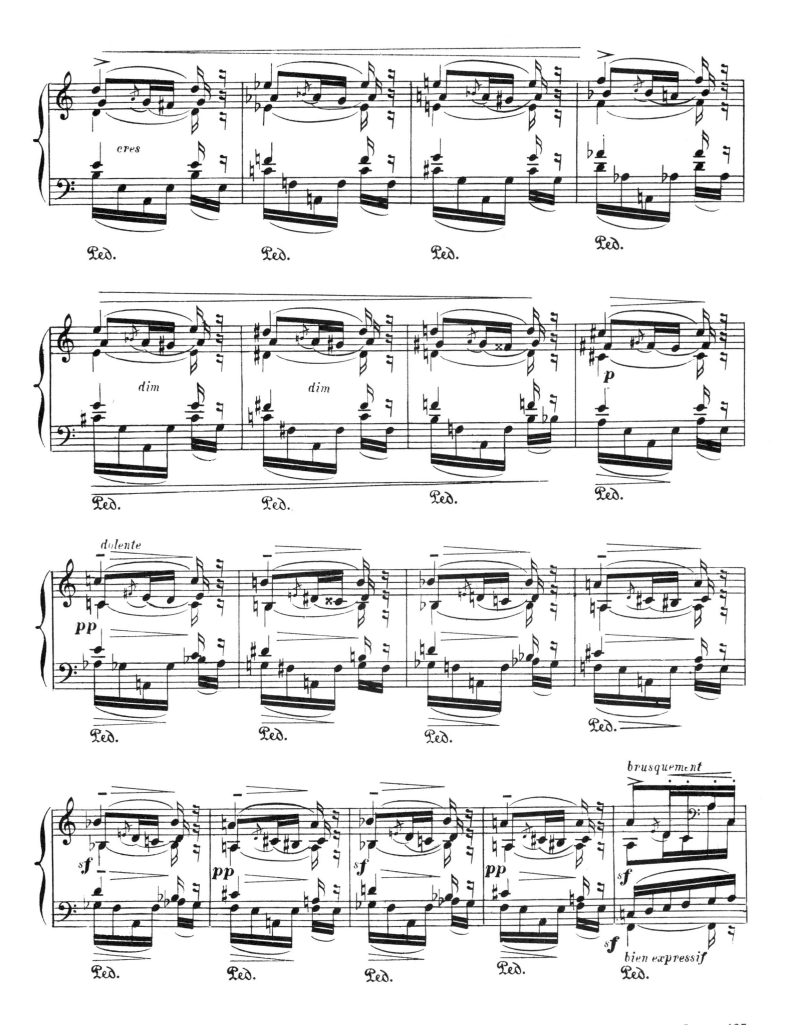

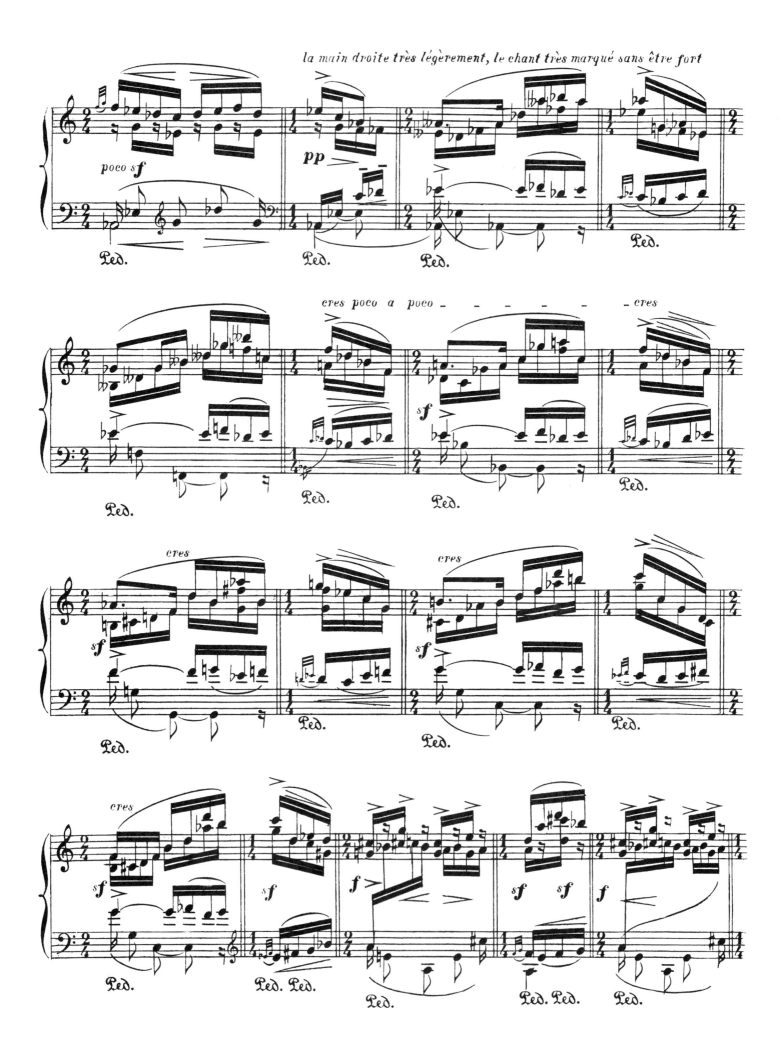

2 mesures en font une antérieure.

ERITAÑA*

*An inn outside the customs gates in Seville.

ESPAÑA

PRELUDIO

TANGO

MALAGUEÑA*

*Spanish dance song with conventional harmonic basis.

SERENATA

*By *rit.*, Albéniz frequently means no more than a passing elongation.

CAPRICHO CATALÁN

ZORTZICO*

*An old Basque dance in quintuple time in which the rhythm is marked on a percussion instrument.